meraki

MERAKI

Tobi-Hope Jieun Park

atmosphere press

For my shikoo 식구: Big Boss, Alpha, forever my guides. My sister, my brother, our pine tree—my best friends, when the world is lonely. My Samchoon and Nana, for giving me so much joy.

For the ones who have helped me see the simplicity of life when the world feels so messy.

For those near and far. Friends past, present, and future. For those who have spoken their lives into me.

For my teachers, who have guided my creativity, encouraged my curiosity, and fostered my faith.

I carry a piece of you in my heart, life, and writing.
Thank you for our time.
Thank you for your love.
Thank you for breathing pulse into my poetry.
Thank you for giving me the most precious gift:
yourselves.

Contents

Meraki • [may-rah-kee]

*to put a piece of yourself into
everything you do*

Persimmon Girl

the orange oval light
which hangs from the tall white pole
makes a big circle on the ground like
gam
After taking its
insides out

Whenever Nana cuts *gam*
she brings
the little knife towards her
over it like a shiny little tractor on a persimmon hill
and whenever she gives a piece to me
my mouth is always sticky
but her hands are always dry

maybe God gives powers to old people
because i think she's like magic

Nana sits right outside of the circle in the dark
on a pile of bricks
while i make myself into the
letters of the alphabet

and i can't help but think that
when im in the streetlight circles
i look like im
wearing a dress of all the orangey skins that
Nana throws away
because i am the persimmon girl.

paraguayo

my father lived amongst the breakings of a
bread factory. as a child, grew strong.
gorged himself on cement glue and barefoot soccer
y el chavo que vivía en un barril por Manzanas.
said, as the telly flickered,
it was his house and now it is mine.
he tells me que su nombre en futbol fue cabbage head.
because his legs were skinny as its thinned roots and
his head was like, yeah.   you know.
 in albums, he is alien, stretching
his features over that bowl of baby skull
and peanut hull. in home, a juicer. at night,
he squeezes the electricity of that native tongue,
presses it into English, and they drink it up like water.

Aladdin at Two

There is no moon and no stars outside,
but it's okay because
Nana turned on a lamp
like someone caught
a little star in a big broken bowl
with white cracks
and
black cracks
and
star cracks
and

Nana's hands look like
Big star leaves
with the squiggles that pop
and
my hands look like
little baby leaf bundles
so when we trade crayons
It looks like two flowers
kissing.

The Freeway Fires

I am five years old.
My family has just moved into our new home.
Our neighborhood is a typical tangle of streets,
except for a wedge of land that squeezes itself between
our street and another.

We discover the
quirks of having a backyard which meshes into
a desert wilderness.
A family of quail explores our pool.
An invasion of toads.

One summer morning, I look out of the window and
the landscape has changed. Usually,
cacti cover the hills, but today
Mustard sprouts have slathered themselves thick
between the saguaro and California shrubbery,
leaving it twinkling and peppery and lemon-dropped.
My father points to a saguaro and tells me
it's at least as old as my grandfather.

In this moment, I'm not sure what sacred is
but I know that this land is something different.
I decide that it is mine.

I am six years old.

I am glued to my Nana's television screen.
There is a monster there.
It is big and orangey-red and hungry and
it isn't picky. It licks the hills before sinking in its

white-hot teeth.
It scorches black bite-marks in its wake.

It is 2008, and we are watching our land burn. I am
afraid. I feel as if i am dissolving,
like paper into fire.

I am twelve years old.
I am writing a poem about the monster,
of hot teeth and scorching tongue and vengeance and
hunger.

The fear has faded. But as I write,
it is clear that the six year old in me has not;
        core still collapsed, body still singed.

Later, my teacher presents us a lesson.
I discover that we live in an area
that sits within the chaparral, a biome
In which fire is natural, restorative,
that the land without burn is a
phoenix without fire,
that the plants cannot grow without
heat and ash.
Though our neighborhoods and homes still bear their
soot scars, that they would
eventually give way to life.
and carefully,
she carves away
stigma and fear and
leaves only understanding.

I am sixteen years old.

Following an early summer shower,
I look out a window
past my backyard
into the land
and i notice something.

Between the cacti, the hills are lemon-dropped. The
mustard sprouts are back.

Four

I.
Today I held out a cob of corn and held hands with an
elephant,
I looked into her eyes and she looked into mine
And for a second I thought she loved me but
She just wanted the corn.

Makes sense.

II.
Once you've seen one rice paddy, you've seen them all.
At least, I think so.
Maybe it's because I don't own one,
But as the Balinese fields ripple past,
I imagine growing rice must be like
Raising children;

Feeding them, cleaning them,
Disappearing on the road.

III.
Some call it sonder,
others a hernia,
I call it a hole right below my heart that fills up with
people but
Never reaches full capacity.
And at parties, I don't lose myself in the music
Because music is a tourist and
my bones ring suburbia

But it does like to nap in my concavities,
Like a cat.

IV.
A pastor once said that if you don't fit in →
not for this world →   the otherworldly =
the bright and beautiful ones
(Be the salt and light, my beloved)
but I beg to differ because
The congregation picks us out with their eyes closed,
Fingers perched like radio antennae

So when I pray,
I mumble in megahertz as a
Signal fire burns through my palms.

the way we fold

In a dream, we rest in the woodpeckered hollow
                                        of a white gumtree,
heels dancing on bleached bark, fingers crooked over
                                        nook's edge,
there is a whole grassland beneath us;
your face glows blushed in the savanna light
        (beautiful as always)

I remember something. Your smile used to be
left handed, like a ripple, young and bluey
and drawn from the dark of a desert well.
        Sweet then, sweet now.
It has since evened out, as water does.

From a shirt pocket, a pair of lungs is procured.
Then another.
They are shiny, sponges, oiled and supple-soft
        (a Trade)
A child would've filled mine with butterflies, but
you are no child, so you stuff them with peacocks
until i am breath-bursting with bright blues
and emeralds and false eyes.

You are delicate,
particular.
Your fingers fold one bird at a time
        (head over wing)
plant them in alveoli and wrap them capillarily.
                                Oh—a present!
And yes, there are quills but only when you are gone.

I don't remember what I gave you. Only that you were

grateful.
      You are always so grateful—graceful—careful.

Thus, we are
      Have you ever watched seeds germinate?
      Of course you have. But we are
juvenile, and I like it that way; shy. tentative.
clumsy-curling during early spring rains

We burst from the loam together.
I am not afraid of you but when we
break the surface/seal the trade/pull apart
you leave me
open-mouthed
      peacock-breathed
          gentle-fished
and even outside of dreams you are
beautiful
as always.

Somnia

And I was there,
fallen,
in the way corporealities do,
and I was like lead (metal). and If not lead, then like
the hand with which a friend can cleave parts of you
away and
pack them up for supper.
Are you ███? Why are you ███?
Your presence settles in my ribs, but the face is
different, like a
smoldering doorstop when idle fingers pluck at it.
You call me by my spirit name
              (you pronounce it correctly)
the lips parted soft-palate-touch which is not present
in mother tongue.
Are your dreams in English? Do you speak
cottonmouth?
The zoysia ripples but I have not forgotten.

Brooke

Dear Sea,

You were like a mother to me,
My childhood salted with
Stories of you, of shores
touched and tasted by
A Nazarite,

You watch the waters
Sever from your surface
Knowing they
Will always return to
Your crystallized palms

Dear River,

You were like a brother to me,
Loud and wild,
You break the laws of border and bank,
Laughter echoing cavernous,
        like stone on stone on stone on stone
and though your shrieks split mountains,
I knew you would never hurt me.

Dear Brooke,

You are a sister to me.

I hold the crook,
The creek of your neck

In my arms
Your heart palpitating
Like spring

You taste of ice and milk,

We can feel you passing over our skins.
The last time an angel passed over, they gave it a name
      (I call it New Year's)
but there is nothing new about the fact that
our hands are now dry,
And the ground is still damp,

Little one,
You have travelled so far from
Here,

Dear Brooke,
Dear River,
Dear Sea,

Dear Mother,

Bring her home.

*thunder is like war in that the sky is on fire and
people are afraid*

We hide in the velvet night and rain but
When ▓ accidentally rustles
The black-out curtains of our hemisphere
As he checks the streets outside
(for broken planes parts)
The white picket fences are on fire

for a second our pupils fill with
burn/light/flash-photography
and
the clouds tremble above us,
Suspended and electrified,

The Little Prince as told by a pilot-in-theory

The Little Prince is a strange boy who never answers questions, with hair as gold as wheat fields, and a penchant for youthful wisdom. One day, as he weeds the baobab saplings from his home asteroid, B-612, he discovers a rose. But as she grows more beautiful, she becomes more demanding, coquettish, and the Prince's love for her tinges with anxiety. So, he escapes via bird migration. After his meanderings to other planets, he lands in the Sahara Desert, where he meets the Pilot.

I The Prince at Six

The lights flicker-open as my father enters the study room. I am tucked under the table, so he kneels to the floor and lays on his belly. He props his body onto his elbows.

The tips of his fingers pull at the blue leather. Pages peel open.

Like gossip, he tells of the Prince's interactions with adults, of the king's desperation, the vain man's foolishness, the tippler's drunken tautology. His words paint adulthood as mundane, lacking color, or light or logic.

My father begins to shrink. I realize that he was only so big because authority stacks inches, and the crown of his head lowers to the under-table troposphere. The pictures amuse me, though I take a deeper interest in the curved grain of the floorboards.

II. L'essentiel est invisible pour les yeux

A documentary glows out from the television,
and I sag, soft-like, against the back cushions. I sink
into the desert that plays across the screen.

    Smooth as scoria:
        grains of sand blow over dunes,
           burn scarlet against the
           blueish sky
        Oprah Winfrey's voice slicks through
           surround sound speakers
           imbedded into the ceiling
              (they look like lights, you know)

Recognition flickers within me, pixelating the scene.
My sister is unscathed.

III. The Prince/The Pilot/I

I bring a sketchbook to church, and instead of
playing, I draw. In the chapter I had read, the Little
Prince requested from the Pilot a drawing of a sheep,
so he could take one back to B-612. . The Pilot could
not manage.
    I thought that surely, because I was a child, I
could draw a better sheep than the Pilot.

    The Pilot's sheep: thin, shaven bare, shivering
between leather covers
    My sheep: bold, rounded at the edges, strong-
legged

I draw more sheep than the Prince could ever maintain. They would've plucked his wheat fields dry.

IV. I had one line in the entire production.

When I perform in our dance studio's enactment of The Little Prince, I am one of many, nine-year old roses. The stage is blackbox, and new, so I unfurl one petal at a time. My umbrella unfurls with them.

There is one rose, and her name is [REDACTED], and she is unique in all the world. When she unfurls, the audience watches her. She is flirtatious, moody, lines bubbling from her lips like a fountain of story.

The rest of us swirl around her in dance, of which I take comfort in its simplicity, its togetherness. We are a dime a dozen. She is one in a million.

I decide I am not a stage person.

V. A Parallelism with the Tippler

The classroom un-flicker-furls, and the whiteboard scrawls with colors. The lesson is utterly unfascinating. The graph paper on my desk is littered with loose-wristed scribbles.

A wraith, graceful and subconscious, taps me on the shoulder, pulling me back from whatever milk-froth-thought I'd drifted into. She is hairless, and eyeless, with long, delicate fingers, and she collects my wanderings into a teakwood bowl.

"What are you doing there?"
"I am daydreaming."
"Why are you daydreaming?"
"So I may forget."
"Forget what?"
"Forget that I am ashamed."
"Ashamed of what?"
"Ashamed of daydreaming!" Even as I think,
my eyes unravel to periphery and I gaze into a space
that does not exist.

VI. I think he is lonely.

The fox, upon meeting the Prince, begs to be
tamed because as a wild fox, he is like any other in the
world. However, if he is to be tamed, he would be
unique in all the world because he would not be a wild
fox, he would be *the Prince's* fox. "You see the grain-
fields down yonder?" The fox tells the Little Prince,
"Wheat is of no use to me. The wheat fields have
nothing to say to me. And that is sad. But you have hair
that is the colour of gold. Think how wonderful that
will be when you have tamed me! The grain, which is
also golden, will bring me back to the thought of you.
And I shall love to listen to the wind in the wheat..."
So, the Prince obliges.
I am reminded of the fox when a friend tells me
that there is no such thing as intrinsic value.

He tells me that:
importance is proportional to rarity

because he is a violist, and an
 Asian one at that, he is not rare.
 Therefore, he is not important.

the fox was like many other foxes,
 unimportant in its foxhood.
 Until the Prince tamed him.
 Until the Prince made the fox his.
 It is the time you have wasted
 for your **[REDACTED]** *that*
 makes your **[REDACTED]**
 so important.
 Thus, the fox was unimportant until
 an external source, (the Prince)
 made it important.

He forgets that:
 the fox begged to be tamed, implying an
 intrinsic potential.
 Potential, by nature, is value.
 he is not a fox, so it doesn't apply to him
 (though I see the resemblance)

VII. Is Anyone Home?

The Little Prince compares his body to a husk,
a shell, and there is nothing sad about a shell, is there?
It is old, and abandoned, and empty.

But is there?

My yearbooks are still inhabited by old
shadows the way naphthalene clings to wool.

Signatures are scrawled thin, occasionally accompanied by notes. I flicker to the first page of my grade's section, and a familiar face stares back at me. It is old, and abandoned, and empty.

Ink unfurls from my hands, and I meticulously circle the face and name. In my best printing, under the photo, I inscribe a date of birth. A quick hyphen. May 2018.

I fall asleep with a Little Prince in my lap.

cello

there is a mercury to the way
a bow coaxes itself. it does so,
so softly.
now, to the hollow mouth: do not be afraid to
cough up a song which slicks of wood. there is only
so much grit you can take.
have you ever burned yourself into the lattice of sinfonia?
because this is how glass is made.
this is where the quaver is scorned.

the easier way to deconstruct a monroe
(by waveform? or otherwise?)

my grandmother says the funny thing about bones is that
the Hip is like a man; it whines and has teeth. He
socketswallowscrapes Femur because
why not? Hip says. don't you want me? Hip says.
see my bluer veins, deeper sinews. Hip displays the
cream of his calcium, collects collagen into cushion.
here, a place for you to sit. now that you've seen
how strong i am, do you love me?
my brother says the funny thing about bones is how
jaggedy they are, but no one sees their
sharpness because of
skin • /skin/ • noun • a bag which collects bones and
shakes them sensual.
Like salamander spawned in the dark of the void
there is something potion about it,
ocean about it,
concealing some sort of darkly emotion about it.
my best friend says that the funny thing about skin is that
we are but pouches filled with clouded wine. over
a glass of tap water, she tells me that everyone
looks good in skin, but she doesn't like the taste of it.
(it's too gamey.) the easier way, you see, to
read someone is to dissolve them in
aerial silks and enamel.
Watch how they move as
we sip from opposite rims.

Oppy

the first thing she remembers is the descent.

Air burns around her, cushions bloom over base.
a tug from her gut, then
pull, parachute, panic.
it is only her first day, and she is already unravelling.

As she touches land,
There is
A quick evaluation. Her body is unscathed,
so she sets out.
As tread touches the rud of oxidation,
particulate slips into her joints but
it's okay.
she's built for this.

We send messages in shards, and she returns the favor
shows us secrets of a world beyond,
of a surface dust-rusted beyond our own,
Of eclipses and trails and
sandstorms and moons

When she passes,
she calls to her scientists. A storm of
Unprecedented magnitude swirls around her.
They know she will not survive this one.

In their eulogies, they refer to her as machine,
or life,
or both.

How human it is to be mourned,
to gain pronoun and name

How human it is to phone home,
as the dark swallows your earth and leaves
you, glass eye,
gaping and blind.

Type II

I hate the way our
skulls fracture like
light thrust into prisms,
photons rattling about between
Crystal lattice
Fluorite-screams

they reopen fontanelles
in my hairline but you are a dyson
Sphere,
locketing around a
pocket of strange matter as we retch
our cores and tremble

we're still not over '92

For Franny Choi's "Choi Jeong Min"

the classroom split,
black on one, white on the other,
Like kitchen magnets forced to kiss
they repelled and I was caught
in the net of their polar-racial fields

> I felt the tattoos of eyes on my skin,
> blinking through black and white grains
> of old Jim Crow Propaganda,
> the teacher pointed at my face,
> mouth shut,
> said:
> "she wouldn't be here
in class,
I ask my teacher,
"Did anything happen in Korea?"
and she tells me,
"Probably, but it's not important."

Korea only existed on pantry shelves and
between my Nana's teeth,
amongst scorched grains of rice in
tupperwares of *nooroongi,*

we never saw Korea in the classroom,
Fingers raised,
Voice projecting-peninsular,

> But all I saw of Africa was a blur on a map
> Butchered by cat o' nine tails

And blanched by the word "negro"
The countless recordings playing on monsoon loop
of black twig legs knee deep in red mud
mud huts in with leaf-shamble roofs.

When I got into the car, I asked,

Mommy, am I black or white?

But I never had that choice,
my whole identity was defined
by a token check-list on a standardized test,
always the antithesis, always the outlier.

But at least you *knew*.
At least you can contain your ancestry to a country.

I'm not Korean.   I'm not African
But I'm not American yet.

Korea says my words swell too loud for my mouth
and I spit out riots,
that grab for the low hanging fruit
and blame the spoiled apples on my
lack of a stepladder.
Korea says slavery is just an excuse.

Black says I am *gumiho,*
fox o' nine tails, worshipper of the
Slippery and sly,
Draw the coins from your pocket and
figures from your bills as I *insah,*

Fingers circling navel,
Black says I am too greedy, too complacent in my own
oppression

But we say
We've lost the tongues of our motherland
but we haven't forgotten the taste of her mouth,
Blood sausage, barbecue, the sting of green onions
fresh from the earth

her Songs are the stars our mothers cook into
the
Bone-broth
to follow home when we are lost,
Which is always because

Our curves are forced into war-jagged frames,
And I hope that when I pull away,
my skin will hold those edges close,
like teeth to a sun-dried date.

Cowritten with Christina Miles

For the Boy of Hollow Bones
and an Avian Heart

I.   i have nothing to Give.

i look into the shadows of a room darkened by 4
am and i'm almost sure that i can see your smile
silhouetted on my hanging clothes. Grey and long, the
shadows on the floor spin themselves skeletal along
the wood floor-panels. i don't remember your voice
but i can feel your name, stale and ash on my
diaphragm, crumbling off my throat.
    Drip,
        drop,
When it seeps through my voice, my teeth
unclasp. my fingertips are empty porcelain.

II.   The Giant Country Part One

Most believe that there are seven seas, but once
upon a time, there was an eighth, and if you sailed into
the far southwestern corner of the globe, they say
you'd find the most beautiful sea in all the world. It
had a surface so clear that it you could barely see it
when it rippled, and the sand below was made of the
tiniest opals and at noon, the prettiest blues and the
most gorgeous purples and the brightest yellows all
stirred together like a storm of light. And at night, the
little minnows came out of the sand and danced
together.
    But one day, there was a rumbling from deep
under the earth. The minnows fled from their
underground homes, and they cried out in terror

until...

POP! When the glittery sand settled, there was a big, fat, lopsided shadow lingering above them.

"That's one giant opal," mumbled one of the minnows, and then the minnows told the groupers, and the groupers told the tuna, and the tuna told the sharks, and thus the one, big, fat, lopsided opal became colloquially known as The Giant Country by all the fish in the eight seas.

III. Comitatus

Inside a room that tastes like old paintbrushes, there is a machine smeared
with popcorn intentions on its glass. Butter crusts its four metal corners, but it's not really butter because it comes in agent-orange packets

Agent, Houston, we have a problem:

Even a thousand napkins cannot pass through an ASB popcorn machine,

but the the oily fingerprints of
last year
And last last year
And last last last year

Litter-linger up to elbows like a jaundiced headache. Though the kernels that poured in never spilled out FDA-approved, we still partook of them. A menial communion is better than none at all.

IV. The Giant Country Part Two

Time relaxes all. At first, the Giant Country was

smooth, and rigid, and strict, but now it curved with contour. A great, big mountain range has pulled itself up in the far northeastern side, but a crystal-rich valley has carved itself out of the belly of the island.

It was barren, too, but soon seabirds overhead
Drip,
           *drop*ped small seeds onto it,
and over time, soft grasses sprouted like the hairs of a baby. And with the soft grasses came golden shrubs, and with golden shrubs came jeweled trees and trees like jewels, and with that the minnows gaped. They are very good at gaping.

V.   They Flee the Corner Table

Right eyes swirl shame while the lefts swirl righteous, but the one that is left is only hit by many half-glances.

Perhaps ignorance is evil, but sometimes he is only a boy. Today he is a boy of thread, as Pride holds him up on his seat like a marionette. Her arms weary as the others flee the corner table.

He unravels a pen that is not his. In minutes, he coaxes two springs and an artery of ink from its shell.
Is it possible to cajole a snail from its home?
They say home is where the heart is, but when you can't count all the points you care about, it's hard to find a good circumcenter to rest your head on. The air spirals around him with their stares. They watch her, too, but she stands firm in the gyre.

she pulls a stool beside him.

We speak.

Fingers tighten.
Shell crack.
she still has the pieces.

VI.   Oceans and Doorways

Amongst the jeweled trees and trees like jewels and fairy grasses, a single, crooked wax-apple tree waves in the breeze. During the winter, its meager crop always fell from its meager branches, and the wax-apple tree imagined a meager wax-apple cider or a wax-applesauce, or wax-apple slices and caramel.

This season, it was different. Two apples clung to her rightmost branch through the spring so in the summer, when the sun finally bloomed warm, they were big, and round, and shining. The tree had grown very attached to them (for she had never had company before) but she could feel them becoming looser on the leaf.

"I don't want you to leave, just yet," she whispered. To her surprise:

"Oh, don't worry, we won't," the wax-apples chortled back. *"We just want to get out. It's cramped in here."*

Suddenly, from her two plump apples burst forth two grown gods, sharing three heads. And thus, the two-headed god Janus and the one-headed god Gwydd were anointed as the leaders of the Giant Country.

VII.   Zero Period

The blacktop pulse faded-number orange in

34

crooked rows, snail-track-slow after rain. Camera rolling, a nod.

Ten minutes ago, her car was crushed like a soda can between a foot and the ground in the middle of a street. Now ten feet move together, united under the religion of desperation that chases and chases and chases

The music prowls about our dance. It moves us across the cement with a tentative thumb. Whisks away.

The muses laugh at our effort. We will never be gods.

VIII.   The Argument

"The Giant Country is for our people, and our people alone!" The one-faced god held a cracked goblet in his right hand, but his dramatic gestures spilled a little wax-apple cider onto the ground. It sizzled. He splayed across the crystal sand, and adjusted his headdress of seagrapes.

The two-headed king laughed dryly. He turned.

"Gwydd," he said, "We have no people. We have only trees and bushes and beetles."
"And that is enough! All those unbirthed of this island is unworthy!"
"According to who?"
"Me of course!"
"But I am a king too," remarked the two-faced king. A small smirk lit up his faces as disappointment crossed Gwydd's. "We must agree on all."

"Ah, shucks," Gwydd's lips fell into a pout.

"How about we make a compromise?" Janus suggested. "Only those who pass a test will be able to--"

"The fastest!" exclaimed Gwydd. "The fastest to get here!"

An eye roll, and a chuckle.

"Fine."

IX.   Track and Field and Everything After

Grass is never a question, only an answer to the primordial call of fly-foot-*fall* or maybe it is a question, like,

"Feet, are you listening?"

The earth is always listening, and when the boy with flight in his eyes and feathers in his hands whispered in her ear,
        she heard.
        She knew he was never hers to keep.
        When he ran, the air blurred. He barely left footprints. The grass was never greener on the other side because he had his eyes set on the sun.

        Dear boy of an avian heart,
            I wish I was there to bid you farewell.
        You deserve nothing but the best.

X.   The First Sunset

"Janus?"

"Hm?"

"The sky is burning."

"I know."

A splash. A boy, soaked with seawater, steps onto the opal. The silhouette of wings open behind him.

"Janus?"

"Hm?"

"Someone's here."

"I know."

"Excuse me, is this the sun?" the boy asks. Janus takes Gwydd's hand in his, and they both smile, one childlike and one less so. The opal glows as the sun tilts into the belly of the night.

Her stars are like porcelain.

Sweet dreams, friend. Rest easy.

Five Things that Taste Sweet but Turn Sour

One. Fruit.
Or more, the idea of it.
An apple is always sweeter in theory
Than between the teeth.
But theory doesn't nourish.

Two. Gossip.
The currency of
Adolescence
A word for a whisper,
Salted by
Burned bridges and
Broken oaths.

Three. Wealth
If I had a penny for every time someone told me that
money wasn't everything
If I had a penny
If I had a nickel
If I had a dime
I'd have a bank account flush with metal disks and
leaflet slips
Stacking hour after hour after hour and ⸺
Wealth is fresh, but time stales.

Four. Revenge
A parasite
nestling
nibbling on
morality
Until it crumbles away
Like glass off a cracked mirror,

Falling piece after piece
And when you finally turn to
See where you've gone

Five. Knowledge.
There is nothing but a
clean sheet begging for
an imprint,
And it can only get better from there.
Yet the distance between Earth and clean
Is
Two bites of the forbidden fruit.
It still tastes sweet,
But now it burns.

Broil

Like a dewdrop perched
on an
Old witch's fingertip,

she slips
ridge →
dip →
ridge →
run
run
runaway

the earth, tense like
an
unborn cough locked in labor,
she eases
it
emerges
stillborn

if you
swaddle home
in a cashmere blanket,
you will
you won't
you will
regret it

the
moon rises
like ashy knees
peeling dusty

from cement

and after
good morning
      good night
         good morning
           good night
            good morning,
                s w ee t hea r   t,
            I've made coffee,

the ridges
unridge
into
limestone cliffside
and
when the blanket
drops
the
dewdrops follow.

they lay us out in hodgepodges

there are so many--we are oiled in the ebon
of these fine nights. these fine shows are a
macaronage of souls;
            they swell the music to swell our hearts,
                 fill us with a blued electricity
                       fold between fingers
it must be that time of year again, because
in the sixth grade, i wanted to be the book of leviticus.
(YOU) slip (ME) between the gold-foiled edges. i
want to know how ritual feels. draw me a line.
carve the piece of me that crosses, carry it away.
make me without defect and make me new.
please.   show me what faith is. and thus,
we are summoned before them all:
                altar call: a clothed voyeurism??
the presentation is supple and glassed over.
when it is my turn, you ask me to read the parts
your mother won't like. the ones oiled to the nude.
honeyed en patisserie.

The Neighborhood

It is the time of night where the dark-clay sky has already trickled through the streets, and has inundated it in full. Today, the clouds stir thin. Light pollution pulses plasti-particulate through the haze. Most people sleep, except for a select few. Most are youth.

I. 736 Beechwood

A girl browses her closet in the dark, fingers flicking in and out of the fabric. In class, she is learning about rhetoric, the art and language of persuasion. She is not yet acclimated to the rhetoric of Milton but she is fluent in the rhetoric of stitchery. She does not search for plot, but for message, for her neurons to light-spark-catch something and hold it to the looking glass.

The girl knows that lace makes her look sickly and thin, like the legs of a newborn gazelle, fresh-slipped from the womb. When she was in the second grade, she wore a lace dress to school. Their faces warped. Now, she realizes that her outfit was a reminder: of a nan's doilies, a posh funeral.

II. 739 Beechwood

A boy who is less of a boy and more of a man, but neither of the two, lays in his bed, phone in hand. His thumbs glide over it, and the screen casts a white square on his face. Headphones curl around his ear. He has something better to do, and nothing better to do. His friends have all gone to sleep by now. He drags his index finger down the page, and a small swirling circle at the top emerges. Once it stops, nothing new emerges. He sighs and switches apps.

III. 741 Beechwood

A girl with craters for eyes bores into a text that swims in the concavity of her sockets. She is tired. She reassures herself. She was supposed to sleep almost two hours ago. The light stings her pupils. She wants to quit, but she doesn't want to, because if she does, she's giving up. Her persistence is her only redeeming quality, but how much of it she has and how much she has slept are proportionally correlated. She loses either way.

IV. 739 Beechwood

The boy who is less of a boy and more of a man puts his phone down beside him. His blankets are crumpled on the floor. It's too hot in his room. He is hungry, and though he doesn't, his belly yawns for food. The boy opens his door, careful to keep it silent. He tiptoes downstairs. He feels his way to the fridge, and he wonders if he could echolocate his way through the halls. He doesn't try; his mother is difficult about those kinds of things.

V. 736 Beechwood

The girl flicks the light switch. It's like a blackout. She wonders what would happen if the sun never came up. She knows the earth would freeze, but before that? Maybe they could find a way to survive. People have always survived. If they could, she could too. She swore that she would emerge from high school unscathed.

VI. 741 Beechwood

The girl with cratered eyes thinks otherwise. As words added themselves to the gyre swimming in her skull, she glares harder.

VII. 739 Beechwood
The glow of the fridge bathes the boy in light, but he slams it shut when he hears footsteps. It is his grandmother. She is wandering downstairs, humming quietly to herself. He ducks behind a cabinet, though he doesn't need to. The darkness covers him enough, and she's near blind.

Her feet shuffle out the rhythm of her husband's heartbeat, a twitch here, a pause here. She knows he is dead, but she doesn't know, and she has something better to do, and nothing better to do. She is old.

IX. 739 Beechwood
The old woman shuffles out of the house, and her grandson silently follows. She grins up at the glowing skies, raising her hands. The air shivers around her palms.

"Hello Moon," she laughs, "I am ready, now."
"But *halmi*," the boy whimpers. "I'm not."

X. 741 Beechwood
The cratered girl remembers an old Korean myth. Before the sun or moon or stars, there were two poor children and their mother. On her way home from a long day at the market, the mother encountered a tiger. The tiger was very hungry, and demanded her rice-cakes in exchange for her life, and though she fed him every last rice-cake she had, the tiger was unsatisfied, and ate her too.

The tiger, still hungry, chased the children up a tree, but was unable to catch them. He left to fetch an ax. The little boy, Dalsun, prayed for a rope to fall from

45

heaven, and (as is the nature of prayers in stories), he was answered. The children then climbed the rope, becoming the sun and the moon.

She looks through the windowblind slats. The moon gun-shines full, tonight. The girl can't help but think that today, the moon looks like the face of an aging woman, splotches of melasma permeating from her cheekbones.

Genesis: A Platonic Love Poem

Genesis 1:1.
In the beginning, God created the heavens
and the earth. I guess good things come in twos,
like shoes, like eyes, like hands. But she says
she doesn't like her hands because her fingers are ugly.
When I ask her why, she says that they're too long;
they remind her of spiders. I don't know how to tell her
how much I love her hands, and that it was good that
all ten of her fingers were perfect
because she cradled the world in them,
And a good cradle always meets at the ends.

Now the earth was formless and empty,
Genesis 1:2,
darkness was over the deep, and the Spirit of God
was hovering over the waters. I like to think that
in the beginning, God was the ultimate soccer mom.
He saw the earth as a glass of wine half-full.
though it was empty, he already knew how it would taste.
Earthy and big, and

God said let there be light and there was light. God saw
the light was good, and he separated
the light from the darkness and if anyone knows,
God knows that when creation leaves your mouth it
fulfills you, but that can't explain why she fills my heart
like chicken soup because
I didn't make her.
She made me.

Genesis 1:5, God called the light "day" and
the darkness "night," but we are eclipses from

different countries. While I see day, she sees dark.
I think it's because she looks from the perspective of a
sunrise beaming into the black-out windows of
sleeping towns

and there was evening, and there was morning –
the first day.

I know that the first hour is always the darkest, but
I promise, morning will come.
And though the sleeping may grumble and
lock their doors,
never let that eclipse your bright because

in the beginning God created the heavens and the earth but
he also created me,
and he created you.

And we both know that good things come in twos.

Epistolary

A series of letters punctuates my cerebra like
bioluminescent plankton along Caribbean shores.
They spark up over time, billowing blue-green in the
early morning; I hear your voices amongst the diatoms.

Dear [ONE],

The faux oak table is bare as bone,
except for
the thousand-paper-crane-ocean flashing
(color)
kaleidescopic over it.

You add another to the flood. Your
fingers (cross-hatch) become a
haphazard Ark, if only
for a moment. You once
told me that
sound weaves your rods thready,
the way
light weaves dust particulate,
particular in taste and tone

Compassion/corruption/collapse encircles your
capillaries,
and you're in desperate need of a vasodilator.

When you finally relax,
the Ark opens. An olive branch returns.

Dear [TWO],

Last seen: June 25th, 2019. 12:09am. *I'll talk to you tomorrow.*

The blanched pixels glow from the dark of my screen. Where light meets shadow, I see your previous lives.

   I.   First life
      A. you are like a mantis, in that:
          1.   your eyes shift,

               compound-pixelated —

          2.   you hunt the other children —
              a)   your walk shybold in residue
          3.   your smile tends to unscrew at the

               corners —

              a)   i tell you it quirks.
      B. Recalling your first day: you
          1.   cleaned your nails w/ your teeth
          2.   washed your eyes w/ salt
  II.   Second Life
      A. you are a cellar spider, in that:
          1.   you lurk in corners like a ghost —
               a)   occasionally, your shirt
                    collar pulls you
                    shadows → edge of the
                    blue lunch table.
          2.   you pluck your brethren from
               dusty corners
              a)   plop them into plastic cups
      B. We were a team, you and I.
          1.   We ran a black market.
          2.   A busy recess

a) I nudge you as I pass by.
b) A vial of live ants slips from my hands and into your sleeve.
   (I) Later, you tell me that they died in the stress of transport.

III. Third Life
    A. I'm still waiting for an answer.

Dear [THREE],

The emptiness in your cheekbones gapes and I am afraid of your pupils. You tell me that when you were five, a woman jumped off of a bridge and burst through your sunroof. The parallel lines on the freeway screamed beneath your car, cat-scratching your chassis to a halt.

I asked you what you remember, and you remember red; a body in your lap. Even now, that memory flicker-flashes. Some days, you call it to your conscious. Other days, you fade from me.

Later that day, you made a box with your fingertips, pressed them against the scarlet of the sunset. *Like that.* You told me to envision it.

I don't think I've ever thought of the clouds as *blood-stained* before.

Dear [FOUR],

The blanket
folds over you like an old coat
Voice mid-femme, pun-laden

I ask you,
"Do you remember [REDACTED]?
I dreamt about ▮ last night."

"Again?"
"Again."

You shift, crook your collar.
Thumb, fore, three, four
grip the blanket's edge and cinch it over shoulders:

"It'll be better when you're older."
I laugh, keep in mind that we always do.
and palm to screen,
I fold her.

Dear [FIVE],

I know that my poems trip you up so
I'll keep it brief. We have a promise. It's old and
weathered thin,
but I keep it tucked under the nail of pinky finger.

For safekeeping, of course.

I hope you've kept it somewhere too.

Dear [SIX],

It's been some time, hasn't it?
You've changed since I last saw
you;
I remember your face, but the remembering is fractured,
now.
your legs are different. They spread uneasy-
equestrian,
Like a newborn giraffe.
This is a new habit,
isn't it? Your
knees were smoother before,
The ink in inkstone;
The burble in blood.

You are not unlikeable,
I can promise you that much. Well,
yes,
Maybe to some—
your chaos is not unfounded.
I know,
Your breaths are
impulsive but your hands are
careful. You could peel words like onions.
Yes, you are still a shapeshifter.

[SIX],
I have asked many questions
of you but
now,
I have a few more:

What's your favorite
color? How is

your/my/our mother?
Have you
made friends with any
butterflies?
What are your seasons like?

Are you still writing?
Are you happy?
Have you found peace?

Have you found yourself caught between molars,
ground into calcium dust
and rebuilding yourself like some
conscientious plaything, like some
hermit crab extracted and
plucking itself from
the sand around it?

Acknowledgments

The journals, magazines, and publications which have made my work possible:

"For the Boy of Hollow Bones and an Avian Heart". Havik, 2020.

"Four". Inlandia: A Literary Journey, 2020.

"Oppy". Inkblot, 2020.

"paraguayo". the underwater railroad, 2020.

"Persimmon Girl". the underwater railroad, 2020.

"the easier way to deconstruct a monroe (by waveform? or otherwise?)".
        Common Ground Review, 2020.

"The Little Prince as told by a pilot-in-theory". Summer Workshop for Young Writers at the Kelly
        Writers House, 2019.
        "The Little Prince as told by a pilot-in-theory". Havik, 2020.

"the way we fold". Inlandia: A Literary Journey, 2020.

"Type II". Inlandia: A Literary Journey, 2020.

"we're still not over '92". Cold Mountain Review, 2020.

"we're still not over '92". the underwater railroad, 2020.

This piece was cowritten with Christina Miles, and meant to be read as a dialogue. The line "her songs are the stars our mothers cook into the bone broth to follow home when we are lost, which is always…" is derived from Franny Choi's "Choi Jeong Min".

About Atmosphere Press

Atmosphere Press is an independent, full-service publisher for excellent books in all genres and for all audiences. Learn more about what we do at atmospherepress.com.

We encourage you to check out some of Atmosphere's latest releases, which are available at Amazon.com and via order from your local bookstore:

In the Cloakroom of Proper Musings, a lyric narrative by Kristina Moriconi

Lucid_Malware.zip, poetry by Dylan Sonderman

The Unordering of Days, poetry by Jessica Palmer

It's Not About You, poetry by Daniel Casey

A Dream of Wide Water, poetry by Sharon Whitehill

Radical Dances of the Ferocious Kind, poetry by Tina Tru

The Woods Hold Us, poetry by Makani Speier-Brito

My Cemetery Friends: A Garden of Encounters at Mount Saint Mary in Queens, New York, nonfiction and poetry by Vincent J. Tomeo

Report from the Sea of Moisture, poetry by Stuart Jay Silverman

The Enemy of Everything, poetry by Michael Jones

The Stargazers, poetry by James McKee

The Pretend Life, poetry by Michelle Brooks

Interviews from the Last Days, sci-fi poetry by Christina Loraine

About the Author

Tobi-Hope Jieun Park is a resident of sunny Southern California, and has been writing since the age of eight. Her poems and narratives have appeared in various journals such as Rattle, Chautauqua Journal, SOLA, Common Ground Review, Cold Mountain Review, and more. Tobi-Hope is a three-time Gold Key winner and a National Gold Medalist at the  Scholastic Art and Writing Awards. In her free time, she can be found singing karaoke with her siblings, tending to her pets One-Eyed Jack and the Lizard Gang, and knitting pieces too small for conventional use.

CPSIA information can be obtained
at www.ICGtesting.com
Printed in the USA
FSHW011333261020

9 781649 219275